MARVELS and MYSTERIES

MYSTERIOUS MONUMENTS

Paul Mason

A⁺

Smart Apple Media

This edition first published in 2005 in the United States of America by Smart Apple Media.

Smart Apple Media
1980 Lookout Drive
North Mankato
Minnesota 56003

First published in 2005 by
MACMILLAN EDUCATION AUSTRALIA PTY LTY
627 Chapel Street, South Yarra, Australia 3141

Visit our website at www.macmillan.com.au

Associated companies and representatives throughout the world.

Library of Congress Cataloging-in-Publication Data

Mason, Paul, 1967-
    Mysterious monuments / by Paul Mason.
    p. cm. – (Marvels and mysteries)
    Includes index.

    ISBN 1-58340-771-5

    1. Monuments—Juvenile literature. 2. Antiquities—Juvenile literature. I. Title.
    CC135.M328 2005
    930—dc22

                                                            2005042863

Edited by Vanessa Lanaway
Text and cover design by Karen Young
Page layout by Karen Young
Maps and illustrations by Karen Young
Photo research by Jes Senbergs

Printed in China

Acknowledgments
The author and the publisher are grateful to the following for permission to reproduce copyright material:

Front cover photograph: *Moai* on Easter Island, courtesy of Photos.com.

Texture used in cover and pages, courtesy of Image Farm.

Corbis, pp. 14, 17, 19, 21, 27, 28, 29; Legendimages, p. 10 (top); Mary Evans Picture Library, p. 25; Photodisc, pp. 9, 12, 22; Photolibrary.com, pp. 7, 10 (bottom), 15, 24; Photos.com, pp. 5, 26; The Travel Site, pp. 16, 20, 23; Werner Forman Archive, p. 18.

While every care has been taken to trace and acknowledge copyright, the publisher tenders their apologies for any accidental infringement where copyright has proved untraceable. Where the attempt has been unsuccessful, the publisher welcomes information that would redress the situation.

CONTENTS

GLOSSARY WORDS

When a word is printed in **bold**, you can look up its meaning in the glossary words box, and on page 31.

TIME

Some of the stories in this book talk about things that happened a long time ago, even more than 2,000 years ago. To understand this, people measure time in years Before the Common Era (BCE) and during the Common Era (CE). It looks like this on a timeline:

2000	1500	1000	500	0	500	1000	1500	2000	2500
		Years BCE			Years CE				

LOST worlds

Scattered around the world are physical reminders of people from the past. For many years, no one understood what these crumbling **monuments** were. To try and explain them, people made up stories about lost magic and **ancient** religions.

What kinds of monuments are there?

There are lots of different kinds of monuments. They include:

- pyramids in steamy American jungles
- forgotten temples in Indian forests
- giant stone circles standing in lonely fields
- huge animal figures carved into the Earth's surface.

Most are very old, often thousands of years old.

From the 1400s until 1860, the ancient city of Angkor Wat lay unknown in the Cambodian jungle. In 1860 it was discovered by a French scientist, Henri Mouhot. Since then, parts of the city have been rebuilt.

4

Understanding the monuments

People have lived near some monuments for hundreds of years. Other monuments have remained hidden from sight and only recently been discovered. Today, **archeologists** have begun to solve the mysteries of who built these monuments and why.

Stone CIRCLES

Location: British Isles and northwest France
Date: from roughly 3000 BCE onward

Among the most mysterious of monuments are stone circles. These strange arrangements of stones have puzzled people for years. Were they the sites of human **sacrifices**? Or perhaps meeting places for ancient religions? Or did they have some other unknown purpose?

Stonehenge

Stonehenge is the greatest of all stone circles. The largest stone is 22 feet (6.7 m) high. Many other stones are almost as big. The outer ring of Stonehenge is made by a ditch and bank. Inside this is a circle of holes called the Aubrey Holes.

⋯⋯ An aerial view of the layout of Stonehenge.

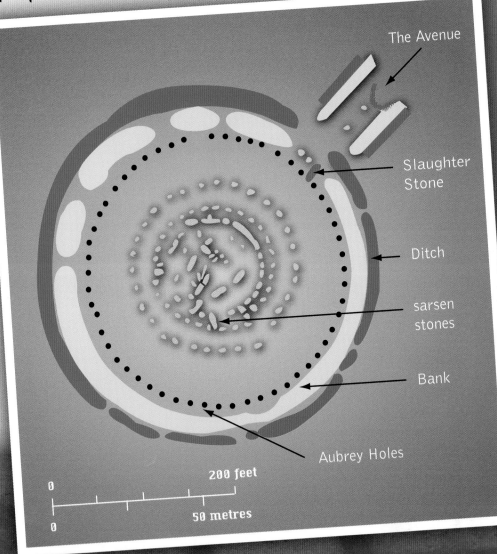

The Avenue

Slaughter Stone

Ditch

sarsen stones

Bank

Aubrey Holes

200 feet

50 metres

0

0

6

Human sacrifice?

Some people have suggested Stonehenge may have been a place of human sacrifice.

- At the bottom of some of the "Aubrey Holes," the burnt bones of human beings were found.

- One of the stones at the entrance to the site is known as the "Slaughter Stone" because of its reddish color.

The tallest stones at Stonehenge are so tall that you would be able to clean a second-floor window while standing on top of one. But as each stone weighs about 33 tons (30 t), it would make a very heavy ladder!

The sarsen stones

The most spectacular part of Stonehenge is the inner circle of giant "sarsen stones." These huge stones weigh an average of 33 tons (30 t) each. Many are arranged in pairs, with a third stone, called a "lintel stone," balanced on top of them. The three stones together are known as a **trilithon**.

GLOSSARY WORDS

sacrifices	gifts to the gods, often made by killing something
trilithon	three stones arranged with one on top of the other two

The mysteries of the stones

The circle builders lived over 4,000 years ago. They did not have modern equipment like cranes, just ropes and their own strength. So how did they bring the stones to Stonehenge, then lift them into position?

Moving the stones

Some of the stones at Stonehenge came from a **quarry** in southwest Wales. How did they travel the 217 miles (350 km) to Stonehenge?

- The stones, which weigh about 4.4 tons (4 t) each, were dragged on rollers or sledges to the sea.

- They were loaded on barges, which floated along the coast, then along rivers to a place near Stonehenge.

- Finally the stones were dragged to Stonehenge.

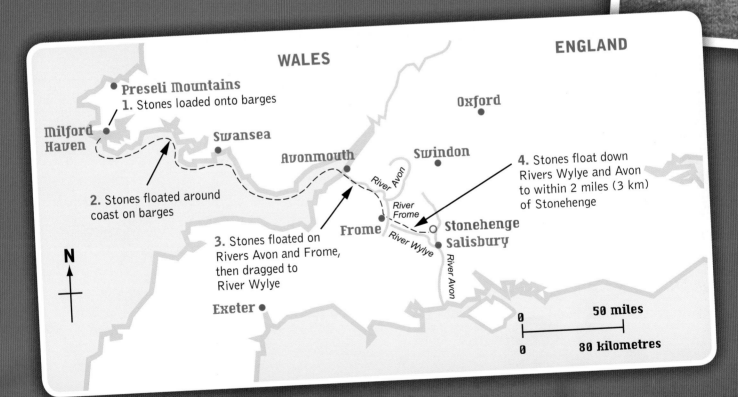

The journey of the 4.4-ton (4-t) "bluestones" from southwest Wales to Stonehenge was an incredible feat thousands of years ago.

Stonehenge has become a popular place for tourists to visit.

Why was Stonehenge built?

Megalithic people used Stonehenge to measure the passing of the seasons. They did this by judging where the sun appeared at the circle's edge at a particular time of day. Most important of all, the stones told them when it was midsummer (the longest day of the year), and midwinter (the shortest day).

FACT FILE

Making a trilithon

Volunteers using only Megalithic-style tools demonstrated how to make a trilithon:

• They dug a hole for the stone to sit in.

• Giant **levers** were used to lift the other end to a 30-degree angle.

• Next, ropes were used to pull the stone upright so that it slipped into its hole.

• Once two stones were upright, ropes and a wooden framework were used to lift the lintel stone into place.

GLOSSARY WORDS

quarry   place where rock or stone is mined from Earth

levers   simple devices for moving heavy loads

Other standing stones

Stonehenge is not the only mysterious stone circle in the world. Most others are in northwestern Europe. But stone circles are found in different countries around the world, such as in Africa and Central America.

"The Druid's Altar" at Drombeg, Ireland.

Standing stones at Callanish, Scotland.

Drombeg, Republic of Ireland

The local people call the stone circle at Drombeg "The Druid's Altar." The Druids were leaders of a religion that existed in the British Isles before the Romans came in 55 BCE. For years people thought the Druids had built the stone circles. We now know that most circles are far older even than the Druids.

Callanish, Scotland

Callanish is on Lewis, a remote island off the coast of Scotland. The stones here are said to be haunted by the "Shining One," who appears on Midsummer's Day. Other stories say the stones are the remains of giants. St Kieran asked the giants to become Christians. When they refused, he promptly turned them to stone.

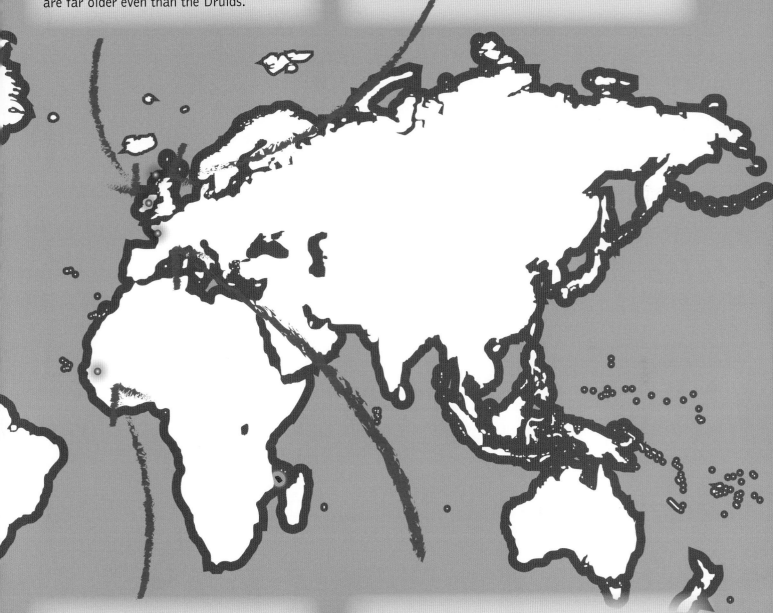

Wasu, The Gambia

Near the Gambia River there are stone circles that puzzled people for years. Now it seems they may be graveyards. A small stone near a bigger one may show the graves of a mother and child, for example.

Carnac, France

The stones at Carnac in France are amazing because of how many there are. Thousands of stones thread the fields and woods, arranged in mysterious lines. The lines look like a long movie line that has been turned to stone. The purpose of the stones at Carnac is still not clear.

PYRAMIDS in Egypt

Location: Giza, Egypt
Date: Great Pyramid built around 2489 BCE

The pyramids of Egypt were one of the **Seven Wonders of the Ancient World**, and are the only Wonder still standing. These giant monuments to the Egyptian rulers, or pharaohs, have stood beside the Nile River for over 4,500 years.

The Great Pyramid, the largest one of all, is roughly 459 feet (140 m) high. The pyramid is built of about 2,300,000 blocks of solid limestone. Each block weighs an average of 2.8 tons (2.5 t). The pyramid was built in an age when people had only simple tools and their own strength to work with.

The Great Pyramid weighs approximately 7,165,015 tons (6,500,000 t). This is the equivalent of 48,148 blue whales (the blue whale is the largest animal that ever lived) all piled up together.

FACT FILE

The Sphinx

The Sphinx guards the entrance to one of the pyramids at Giza.

- The Spinx has the head of a pharaoh and the body of a lion.

- It is over 4,500 years old.

- It is 187 feet (57 m) long and 66 feet (20 m) high.

Why were the pyramids built?

The pyramids were probably the burial places of pharaohs, rulers of Ancient Egypt. The pharaohs were thought to be gods, so it was fitting that they were buried in marvelous monuments when they died. Stories say that the pyramids contained fabulous treasures. Tomb robbers had raided all the pyramids by about 1000 CE.

Pyramid-building tools

The pyramid builder's tools included:

- chisels and mallets for shaping stone

- butterfly clamps, which were bow-shaped pieces of wood used to hold two blocks of stone together

- polishing blocks, pieces of smooth stone used for polishing.

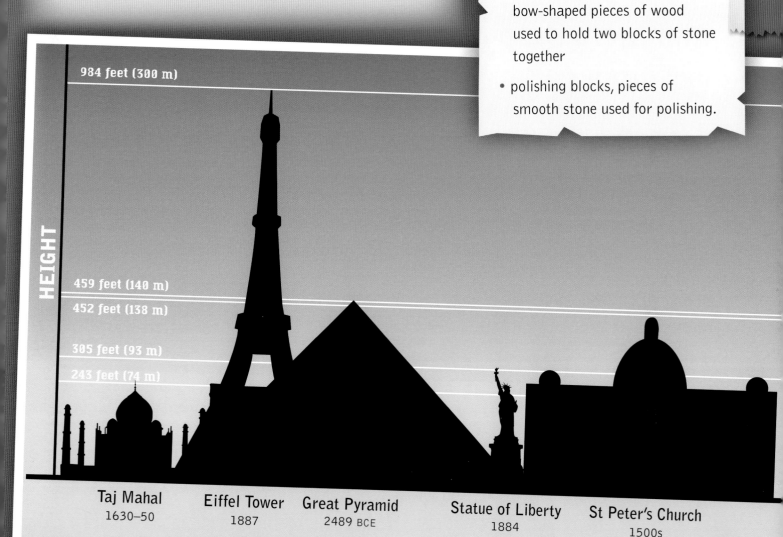

984 feet (300 m)

459 feet (140 m)

452 feet (138 m)

305 feet (93 m)

243 feet (74 m)

HEIGHT

| Taj Mahal | Eiffel Tower | Great Pyramid | Statue of Liberty | St Peter's Church |
| 1630–50 | 1887 | 2489 BCE | 1884 | 1500s |

MONUMENTS

Until the Eiffel Tower was finished in 1887, the Great Pyramid was the tallest structure ever built.

GLOSSARY WORDS

Seven Wonders of the Ancient World seven marvelous sites listed by travelers in ancient times as the places most worth visiting

Who built the pyramids?

A mixture of skilled and unskilled workers built the pyramids. About 4,000 people worked on the Great Pyramid all year round. When the Nile flooded for three months each year, farmers could not work in their fields. They were put to work on the pyramid instead. Even so, it took 20 years to build.

What were the pyramids like inside?

The pyramids contained rooms filled with great treasures of gold and jewels. Many things were done to stop tomb raiders from stealing the treasure. For example:

- the entrances were hidden

- false passageways led to dead ends

- other passageways were sealed with huge "plugs" of stone.

Despite this, every single pyramid was **looted** by tomb raiders.

Egyptian punishments

Tomb raiders were punished with death. But the Ancient Egyptians had different punishments in store for other criminals.

- **Corrupt** officials had their noses and ears cut off.

- Lesser crimes meant working in a labor camp, digging canals, or quarrying rock.

•••••▶ Porters carry a throne from Tutankhamen's tomb. The throne is covered with precious jewels and solid gold ornaments.

How were tomb raiders punished?

Tomb raiders ran great risks. If they were caught, they could suffer terrible punishments. Tomb raiders might be burned alive, or **impaled** on a sharp wooden stake and left to die. Nonetheless, many thought it was worth the risk.

Treasures of the tombs

Tomb raiders never discovered the pharaoh Tutankhamen's tomb. The tomb contained:

- a golden death mask

- three coffins, one made of solid gold and weighing 243 pounds (110 kg)

- over 200 pieces of jewelry.

The portrait mask that covered the pharaoh Tutankhamen's head is made of solid gold and weighs 22.5 pounds (10.2 kg).

GLOSSARY WORDS

looted	stolen, usually as part of a war
corrupt	dishonest
impaled	pierced through with a sharp, pointed object

Riddles of the pyramids

We do not know everything about the pyramids. Since discovering how to read **hieroglyphics** in 1822, we have been able to read the writing carved on pyramid walls or found on ancient fabrics inside. But some mysteries still remain.

The lost pyramids

There are over 30 major pyramids that we know about, apart from the Great Pyramid at Giza. Some have only recently been found. For example, in 1951 the "Lost Pyramid" was discovered buried under the sand. It was built for Sekhemkhet, a pharaoh who was almost unknown until his tomb was discovered. There may still be other pyramids buried in the desert, waiting to be found.

LOCATION FILE

Location: Memphis, Ancient Egypt

Founded: 3100 BCE

Famous because: Memphis was the main port and **capital** of Egypt until the 300s BCE. Most pharaohs built their tombs nearby, at Giza.

The giant stone pillars at Karnak were put up for the pharaoh Thutmose III, who ruled Egypt from about 1490-1436 BCE. Wall carvings tell of his great military victories.

For years experts have known about shafts carved deep into some pyramids. They thought these were meant to carry air inside. But now some researchers claim that the shafts pointed at major stars, which represented Egyptian gods.

The mystery of the mummies

No whole **mummy** has ever been found inside a pyramid, but parts of mummies have been discovered. This makes experts think that the mummies were cut up and stolen by tomb robbers. What no one can be sure of is why the mummies were stolen, or where they went.

GLOSSARY WORDS

hieroglyphics — the Ancient Egyptian writing system

capital — the city where the government of a country is based

mummy — a dead body that has been preserved so it will not rot away

PYRAMIDS in America

Location: southeastern Mexico and Central America

Dates: 300–900 CE (Mayas); 1400s to early 1500s (Aztecs)

Hundreds of pyramids stand in the steamy jungles of Mexico and Central America. Many are yet to be explored. Travelers first began to discover these amazing monuments to lost civilizations in the 1800s.

Who built the pyramids?

Many different groups of people built pyramids in the region. The two greatest pyramid builders were the Mayas and the Aztecs. The Mayas built the Pyramid of the Sun at the city of Teotihuacan. Its base is almost the same size as the Great Pyramid at Giza, but it is only half as tall.

LOCATION FILE

Location: Monte Albán, Mexico

Date: 600 BCE–800 CE

The Zapotec people lived in this region. They built a city of pyramids that were used as temples and tombs. Each tomb had a **niche** where people's remains were stored.

 Zapotec Pyramid of the Niches, El Tajin, Veracruz, Mexico.

What were the pyramids for?

Many pyramids were temples. They had flat tops where religious ceremonies were performed. These ceremonies included human sacrifices. Only priests and rulers were allowed on the pyramid steps. The ordinary people had to wait at the bottom.

Spanish conquerors reached the center of the Aztec city Tenochtitlán in 1519. They were horrified by the stench of blood coming from the pyramids, where thousands of people were sacrificed each year.

FACT FILE

The Aztecs believed that human sacrifice was necessary to keep the universe in order. Sacrifices took place at the tops of pyramids.

- Thousands of victims a year were killed.
- Victims' hearts were cut out while still beating.
- The bodies were thrown down the pyramid steps, then the arms and legs were chopped off and eaten.

GLOSSARY WORDS

niche   a small, narrow space

19

The NAZCA Lines

Location: Nazca Plain, Peru
Date: 200 BCE–400 CE

The Nazca Lines are a monument to the Nazca people, who lived in Peru 2,000 years ago. They are mysterious lines in the surface of the desert, still visible today. Some lines are straight, others curved. But what are the lines, and why are they there?

What are the Nazca Lines?

The Nazca Lines have to be seen from the air to become clear. Dead-straight lines connect mounds on the plain. Curved lines make shapes, including animals and birds. The mystery is, how did the Nazca people make the lines and shapes when they could not fly into the air to see them?

FACT FILE

Ancient UFOs?

- In the 1960s and 1970s, it was suggested that the Nazca Lines had been created with the help of UFOs.

- The drawings were "signals" to UFOs, and the straight lines were "runways."

No evidence has ever been found to prove these ideas.

From the ground, the shape of the Nazca Lines is unclear. They can only be seen clearly from the air. For years people wondered how they could have been created 2,000 years ago.

Why were the Lines made?

The Nazca Lines were once thought by some people to be landing strips for UFOs! In fact, they are almost certainly a giant guide to the skies. The straight lines point at important **astronomical** points, such as where the sun sets at midwinter. The mounds are viewing points.

LOCATION FILE

Location: Kentucky, U.S.

Date: 1982

Joe Nickell and helpers recreated one of the Nazca figures, a giant condor. They used only a small drawing of the condor, long strings, and simple mathematics. This proved that the Nazca would not have needed help from UFOs to create the Lines.

These Nazca lines show a hummingbird.

GLOSSARY WORDS

astronomical   to do with the sun, moon, stars, and other heavenly bodies

The LOST CITY of the INCA

Location: Machu Picchu, Andes Mountains, Peru
Date: built circa 1438

High on a ridge in the Andes Mountains lies the lost city of Machu Picchu. The Inca people who built it abandoned the city in about 1532. It lay hidden, slowly being reclaimed by nature, until 1911.

The Inca people controlled a giant empire. The empire grew as the Inca's powerful armies defeated surrounding groups of people. The Inca usually allowed the rulers they conquered to stay in power. But the rulers had to agree to obey the Inca and pay them taxes.

> All ordinary Inca people had to pay taxes. They might have to give up some of their crops, weave cloth, or go and work for the government. Taxes like these would have helped the Incas to build Machu Picchu.

The Inca people

Life for the Inca people was very strictly organized. Most important were the emperor, his relatives, and the other **nobles**. Least important were the ordinary people. People could only change to a higher rank by performing some great task for the emperor. Almost everyone stayed the same rank for life.

FACT FILE

Inca emperors

Just three men led the growth of the Inca Empire.

- The emperor Pachacuti defeated a neighboring people in 1438.

- His son, Topa Inca Yupanqui, expanded the empire northwest and south.

- Yupanqui's son, Huayna Capac, expanded the empire farther.

- Capac's son, Atahualpa, became the last emperor just in time to be executed by Spanish invaders!

Pilcocayna, the Incan temple of the Sun God. Priests were very important to the Inca. People hardly made any decisions without asking a priest to make a **divination**. This was an attempt to find out what the gods wanted done.

FACT FILE

Inca facts

- The Inca had no writing system. They recorded information on knotted strings with different colors.

- The Inca had no money system.

- Bad illnesses were treated by trepanning—cutting away a piece of skull to let out the sickness.

GLOSSARY WORDS

nobles — people born to a high rank in society

divination — trying to see the future through physical signs, such as how a piece of wood burns or which birds fly past

What was Machu Picchu for?

Machu Picchu was probably a resort for the emperor and his family. Guests from the capital, Cuzco, were entertained in Machu Picchu's great palaces. Smaller buildings nearby were homes for the farmers, weavers, and servants who worked for the royal family.

Why was Machu Picchu abandoned?

No one knows for sure why Machu Picchu was abandoned. The Incas did not write, so there are no records to tell us what happened. But the city seems to have been deserted not long after the arrival of Spanish **conquistadors** in 1532.

The Inca royal family was destroyed when Spanish invaders arrived. Perhaps Machu Picchu was abandoned because there was no one left to stay at the royal city.

Atahuelpa was the last Inca emperor. The Spanish captured him and demanded a **ransom** of one room full of gold and two rooms full of silver. The ransom was paid, but the Spanish killed Atahuelpa anyway.

PEOPLE FILE

Hiram Bingham

Lived: 1875-1956

Description: Bingham was born in Hawaii. He married the **heiress** to a great fortune, became a famous explorer, and later became a senator for the state of Connecticut in the U.S.

Famous for: Hiram Bingham discovered Machu Picchu in 1911.

Who discovered Machu Picchu?

An American named Hiram Bingham discovered Machu Picchu in 1911. He returned from an expedition with tales of the lost city and the Incas:

- Inca rulers had worn cloaks of bat skin.
- Stonework shrines were covered with gold.
- Silver was called "tears of the moon" and gold was called "sweat of the sun."

Having been unknown for nearly 400 years, Machu Picchu was suddenly more famous than ever.

GLOSSARY WORDS

conquistadors Spanish soldiers in the Americas, especially in the 1500s. The word conquistador means "conqueror."

ransom a price paid to set a prisoner free

heiress a woman who inherits the wealth of a relative when they die

The EASTER ISLAND statues

Location: Easter Island, Pacific Ocean
Date: Settled from about 400 CE
onward. Statues made 1400–1600 CE

The first Europeans to reach Easter Island arrived on Easter Day, 1722. They must have been amazed at the sight that greeted them. Littered across the island were giant statues of mythical humans, weighing as much as 176 tons (160 t).

The islanders called the statues *moai*. On average they weigh about 13.8 tons (12.5 t) each and are 13 feet (4 m) high. Even today, moving these huge pieces of rock would be tricky. We now know that it took the islanders years to quarry each *moai*, move it to its resting place, and stand it up.

Why were the statues put up?

The statues probably represent important Easter Island chiefs from the past. They were monuments to these dead leaders. Whole villages would have worked for years on each *moai*. Work would stop when crops had to be harvested or planted, then start again when people had free time.

Many of the *moai* wore "hats" of stone cylinders. These were sometimes painted red.

Moai statistics

FACT FILE

- The average *moai* was 13 feet (4 m) tall and weighed 13.8 tons (12.5 t).

- The largest *moai* ever put up was 33 feet (10 m) tall and weighed 83 tons (75 t).

- The smallest *moai* is just 3.71 feet (1.13 m) tall.

- There are 887 *moai* on Easter Island.

Many *moai* were arranged in groups called *ahu*. They stood together with their backs to the sea.

How were the *moai* moved?

No one knows for certain how the statues were moved. In 1998 a group of experts attempted to move and stand up a replica *moai*. They tried moving it using log "rollers" underneath the statue. The team also tried dragging the statue on a sledge. They used the trunks of banana plants to make the sledge slide more easily.

Easter Island is the most isolated **inhabited** place on Earth. To the east, the coast of Chile is 2,300 miles (3,701 km) away. Tahiti is 2,500 miles (4,023 km) northwest. The closest land is Pitcairn Island, 1,400 miles (2,253 km) to the west.

MINI FACT

Easter Island is a tiny speck in the middle of the Pacific Ocean. The original settlers did not have modern navigational tools. They would have used the stars, winds, and ocean currents to find the island.

Destruction of the moai

Easter Island became increasingly crowded throughout the 1500s and 1600s. Eventually there was not enough land to go around. A **civil war** began in about 1680, as people fought for space.

When the war ended, the winners began to topple the statues. They continued doing this for the next 150 years. Most *moai* were pulled to the ground and had their necks broken. Today about 15 *moai* have been put back in their original places.

Pacific explorers

Polynesian people traveled vast distances as they journeyed in search of new lands:

- Around 400 CE Easter Island was settled.

- By about 600 CE Hawaii had been reached.

- In about 800 CE the first voyagers reached New Zealand.

Easter Island was once full of forests and rich land. By the time the civil war started in about 1680, the forests had been cut down, partly to help in moving and putting up the *moai*. The land had become bare.

GLOSSARY WORDS

inhabited   lived in by people

civil war   a war between members of the same country or community

TIMELINE

4000–1500 BCE	Megalithic people build stone circles in northwest Europe.
3000 BCE	Work begins on the stone circle at Stonehenge, England.
2650 BCE	The first-ever pyramid, at Saqqara in Egypt, is built. It was designed by Imhotep, who 2,000 years later was worshipped as a god of wisdom by the Ancient Egyptians.
2489 BCE	The Great Pyramid at Giza, Egypt is built.
600 BCE–800 CE	Zapotec people in Mexico build pyramids to use as tombs and temples.
200 BCE–400 CE	Nazca people in Peru leave behind mysterious lines carved in the surface of the desert.
300–900 CE	Mayan people build pyramids as temples, used for human sacrifice, in Mexico.
400 CE	Polynesian voyagers reach Easter Island in the Pacific Ocean.
750 CE	Stone circles at Wasu, near the Gambia River, are built.
800–1000 CE	The first settlers arrive in New Zealand/Aotearoa.
1400–1600 CE	Aztec people in Mexico and Central America build pyramid temples. Like the Mayans before them, they use their pyramids for human sacrifice. Easter Islanders make giant *moai* statues of their ancestors: one day almost 900 will fill the 64-square-mile (166-sq km) island.
1438 CE	About this time, work began on the hidden city of Machu Picchu in the Peruvian Andes.
1532 CE	Spanish soldiers reach the Inca Empire in South America, rapidly defeating the Inca armies. Inca society soon collapses.
1722 CE	Jacob Roggeveen, a Dutch explorer, is the first European to set eyes on Easter Island.
1822 CE	Jean-Francois Champollion discovers the secrets of the Rosetta Stone and learns how to read Ancient Egyptian writing.
1911 CE	U.S. explorer Hiram Bingham discovers the lost city of Machu Picchu in Peru.

GLOSSARY

ancient very old

archeologists people who study ancient people through the things they have left behind

astronomical to do with the sun, moon, stars, and other heavenly bodies

capital the city where the government of a country is based

civil war a war between members of the same country or community

conquistadors Spanish soldiers in the Americas, especially in the 1500s. The word conquistador means "conqueror."

corrupt dishonest

divination trying to see the future through physical signs, such as how a piece of wood burns or which birds fly past

heiress a woman who inherits the wealth of a relative when they die

hieroglyphics the Ancient Egyptian writing system

impaled pierced through with a sharp, pointed object

inhabited lived in by people

levers simple devices for moving heavy loads

looted stolen, usually as part of a war

Megalithic a time when people built monuments with giant stones

monuments buildings or structures that are a reminder of past people or events

mummy a dead body that has been preserved so it will not rot away

niche a small, narrow space

nobles people born to a high rank in society

quarry place where rock or stone is mined from the Earth

ransom a price paid to set a prisoner free

sacrifices gifts to the gods, often made by killing something

Seven Wonders of the Ancient World seven marvelous sites listed by travelers in ancient times as the places most worth visiting

trilithon three stones arranged with one on top of the other two

INDEX